Country Music Stars

TIM McGRAW

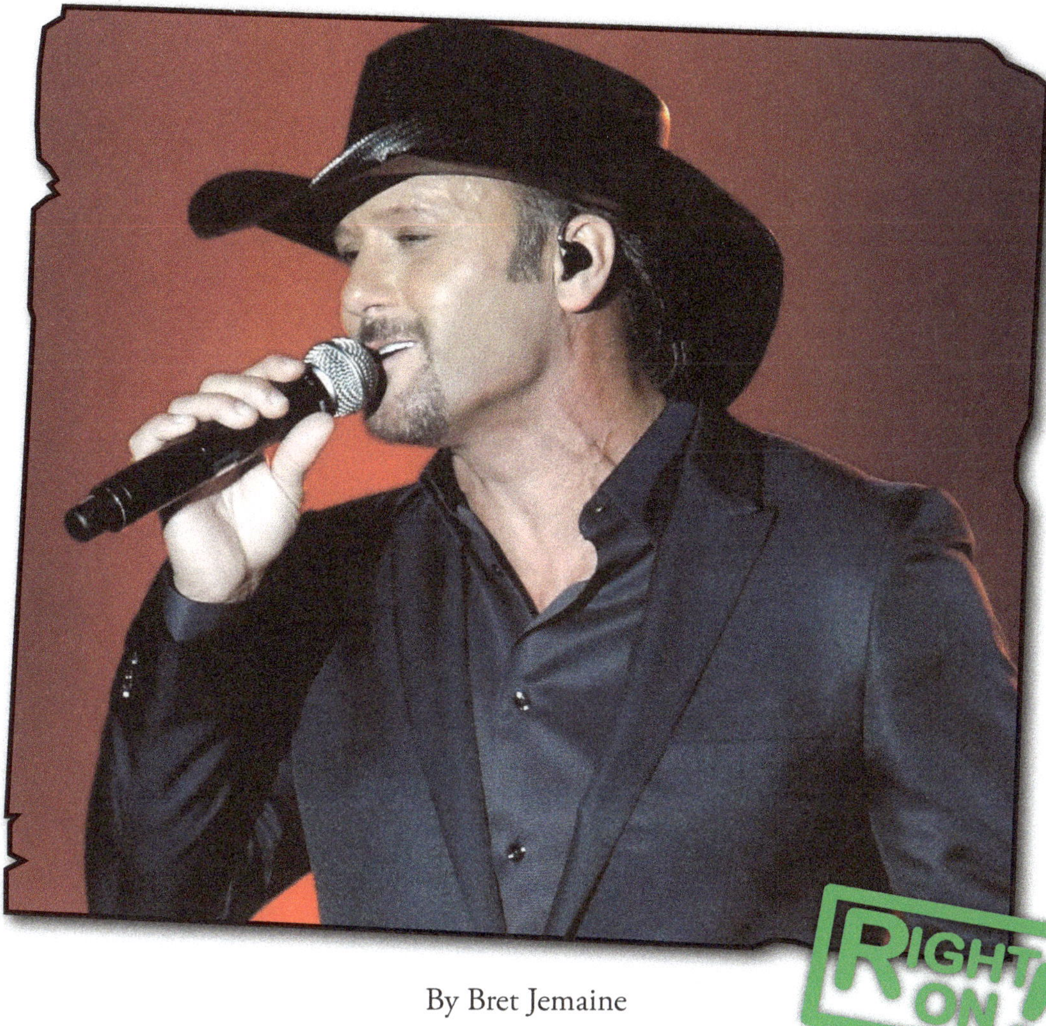

Right On!

By Bret Jemaine

Please visit our Web site, www.garethstevens.com. For a free color catalog of all our high-quality books, call toll free 1-800-542-2595 or fax 1-877-542-2596.

Library of Congress Cataloging-in-Publication Data

Jemaine, Bret.
Tim McGraw / Bret Jemaine.
p. cm.—(Country music stars)
Includes index.
ISBN 978-1-4339-3942-6 (pbk.)
ISBN 978-1-4339-3943-3 (6-pack.)
ISBN 978-1-4339-3941-9 (library binding)
1. McGraw, Tim—Juvenile literature. 2. Country musicians—United States—Biography—Juvenile literature. I. Title.
ML3930.M38J46 2011
782.421642092—dc22
[B]

2010010177

First Edition

Published in 2011 by
Gareth Stevens Publishing
111 East 14th Street, Suite 349
New York, NY 10003

Copyright © 2011 Gareth Stevens Publishing

Designer: Haley W. Harasymiw
Editor: Therese Shea

Photo credits: Cover (background) Shutterstock.com; cover (Tim McGraw), pp. 1, 17 Ethan Miller/Getty Images; p. 5 Bryan Bedder/Getty Images; p. 7 Thomas S. England/Time Life Pictures/Getty Images; p. 9 Adriane Jaeckie/Getty Images; p. 11 Rick Diamond/Getty Images; p. 13 Lawrence Lucier/Getty Images; p. 15 Bryan Bedder/Getty Images; p. 19 Frank Micelotta/Image Direct; p. 21 Carlo Allegri/Getty Images; pp. 23, 25 Scott Gries/Getty Images; p. 27 Stephen Lovekin/Getty Images; p. 29 Hector Mata/AFP/Getty Images.

All rights reserved. No part of this book may be reproduced in any form without permission in writing from the publisher, except by a reviewer.

Printed in the United States of America

CPSIA compliance information: Batch #CS10GS: For further information contact Gareth Stevens, New York, New York at 1-800-542-2595.

CONTENTS

TIM THE SUPERSTAR

Tim McGraw is a musician and actor.

He is a superstar of country music.

MUSIC AND BASEBALL

Tim was born on May 1, 1967. His full name is Samuel Timothy McGraw. His father was baseball player Tug McGraw.

Tim McGraw
Tug McGraw

Tim grew up in the town of Start, Louisiana. He liked to ride in his stepfather's truck. Tim sang along with the radio.

Tim played baseball in college. He also learned to play the guitar. Tim was not happy in school.

Tim left college to start his music career. In 1989, he moved to Nashville, Tennessee.

At first, Tim played and sang at small clubs. He began working with a record company in 1992.

Tim's first song came out in 1992. It was called "Welcome to the Club."

Tim's first album was not a big hit. However, his second album was the best-selling country album in 1994. It was called *Not a Moment Too Soon.*

TIM AND FAITH

Tim's next album was *All I Want*. In 1996, he went on tour with country music star Faith Hill.

Tim and Faith married. They began singing together. "It's Your Love" was one of their biggest hits.

In 2006, Tim and Faith went on tour again. It was the most successful country music tour ever.

MORE ABOUT TIM

Tim is also an actor. In 2009, he starred in a movie called *The Blind Side*. He has acted on television, too.

BASED ON THE EXTRAORDINARY TRUE STORY

Tim has also written a children's book called *My Little Girl*. What will he do next?

TIM McGRAW
HOLLYWOOD WALK OF FAME

TIMELINE

1967 Samuel Timothy "Tim" McGraw is born on May 1.

1989 Tim moves to Nashville, Tennessee.

1992 Tim's first song comes out.

1994 *Not a Moment Too Soon* is the best-selling country album.

1996 Tim marries Faith Hill.

2006 Tim and Faith go on the most successful country music tour ever.

2009 Tim stars in the movie *The Blind Side*.

FOR MORE INFORMATION

Books:

Adams, Michelle Medlock. *Tim McGraw*. Hockessin, DE: Mitchell Lane Publishers, 2007.

Wooten, Sara McIntosh. *Tim McGraw: Celebrity with Heart*. Berkeley Heights, NJ: Enslow Publishers, 2010.

Web Sites:

Tim McGraw
www.timmcgraw.com

Tim McGraw: Biography
www.cmt.com/artists/az/mcgraw_tim/bio.jhtml

Publisher's note to educators and parents: Our editors have carefully reviewed these Web sites to ensure that they are suitable for students. Many Web sites change frequently, however, and we cannot guarantee that a site's future contents will continue to meet our high standards of quality and educational value. Be advised that students should be closely supervised whenever they access the Internet.

GLOSSARY

career: a person's job

club: a place where music is played and people dance

college: a school after high school

musician: a person who sings, plays, or writes music

record company: a business that produces and sells music

tour: a trip to many places in order to play music for people